AMISH LIFESTYLES

AMISH LIFESTYLES
ILLUSTRATED

Illustrated and Written
by Terry L. Troyer

a TLT Publication

AMISH LIFESTYLES ILLUSTRATED

Library of Congress Catalog Card Number: 82-90105

ISBN: 0-943314-00-3

TLT Publications
202 South Fifth Street
Goshen, Indiana 46526

Printed in the United States of America

To Cynthia,
my wonderful wife
and best friend.

ACKNOWLEDGEMENTS

I thank the Lord for the ability and opportunity He has given me to illustrate and write *Amish Lifestyles.*

Many people helped to make this book possible. Some were inspirational and some provided valuable information or editorial assistance. I am indebted to LeRoy and Phyllis Troyer, Cynthia Troyer, Eugene and Orpha Schertz, Tilman Smith, John McCaffrey, Joel Cooper, Jean DeBaets, Mary LeMon and a special thanks to my Amish grandparents, Seth and Nancy Troyer.

PREFACE

I maintain a strong interest in the Amish because they are a part of my background and heritage.

I have respect for the Amish and their constant devotion to God and Christ which is chiefly illustrated by the simple lifestyles they lead.

As "backward" as they may seem to society today, there is much we can learn from their close-knit families, the communities they maintain, their conservative way of life, and their love and stewardship of the land around them.

It is ironic that in the midst of high technology and a hurried world the Amish have survived and prospered. As a result of their close family unity, they have remained strong.

There are many misconceptions regarding the Amish and their beliefs. I feel there is a need to present them in a simplified manner so that the layperson may obtain a clear and correct knowledge of them. And, since my talents lie much more in drawing rather than in writing, I have chosen to do this "sketch book" on the Amish.

INTRODUCTION

THE OLD ORDER AMISH

These gentle and quaint people in the United States and Canada conform to traditions and beliefs based on an historic biblical interpretation which stresses separation from the world culturally and physically as much as possible. The Amish do not expect others to follow their practices, but they do want to maintain their freedom to follow the beliefs of their forefathers, thus instructing their children in such a manner that they will choose to live and die in the Amish faith.

The Old Order Amish, generally referred to as Amish, are farmers or those who follow related careers which permit them to live in an Amish community close to the soil. Their life styles are simple, and, individually or as a Brotherhood, they are able to meet their needs of food, clothing, shelter, transportation, education, religious training, security, and caring for their elders reasonably free from worldly dictates.

ROOTS

Historical libraries and other genealogical sources are experiencing a tremendous increase in research today. Many types of processes and networks are being developed enabling researchers and interested persons to learn more about their family trees, roots of institutions, and various programs. Even first graders are coming to grandparents with genealogical assignments from their teachers to help trace the family trees of "grandmas" and "grandpas" as far back as possible. This is not the beginning of a new wave of "ancestor worship" but an awakening which recognizes roots are important, and knowing one's history helps us understand who we are and what we could become.

Many persons today of all age groups are concerned for the future and are activated by the threat of a nuclear holocaust. This uncertainty may contribute to their interest in knowing more about the abiding values which helped their parents and grandparents meet the issues and demands of their day.

Terry L. Troyer, the author of this book, is a young man with such interests. His paternal grandparents are members of the Amish church. Terry appreciates his heritage, and he understands and loves his Amish grandparents and their lifestyles.

He believes that the Amish have something to teach us today about values which do not change. In a recent letter he stated:

> I have deep respect for the Amish: their devotion to God, their simple life. Although they may seem to be backward in the eyes of some, there is much we can learn from their close-knit family life, their well kept facilities and premises, their love for the soil and the stewardship thereof, their care and respect for their elders, and the strong desire to stay clear of govern-

mental dependence, including Social Security.
They care for their own and are also willing to
help their neighbors.

Others world wide have reached the conclusion that, in
a world of limited resources, there must be people like the
Amish to point out to the rest of us how to care for God's
creation and how to demonstrate love, humility, and fulfill-
ment of human relationships as the quiet of the land.

THE AMISH SPRANG FROM THE MENNONITES

To many persons in North America and elsewhere, it seems
the Old Order Amish are just now being discovered. The
Amish are not a new sect which have reverted to life styles of
a century or more ago; their roots go back to the Reformation period and the Anabaptists, or Mennonites, whose origin
is dated 1525.

Increased media publicity together with numerous research
studies have popularized and drawn attention to the Amish,
thus bringing about increased confusion regarding these
gentle people. Mennonites are called Amish, and Amish are
called Mennonites; and many persons today, adhering to the
Anabaptist faith, are not certain of their historical roots.
Thus, it comes as no surprise that the general public is unable
to sort out the different strains.

The story of the Amish should be told. Therefore, Mennonite and Amish historians have delineated a somewhat
coherent chronicle of Anabaptist beginnings and the source of
Amish faith and life.

THE REFORMATION

The sixteenth-century religious movement which arose in
order to modify practices of the Catholic Church in Europe
has come to be known as the "Reformation."

Certain religious leaders in the early sixteenth century
believed that the Catholic Church was too legalistic, too
irrelevant, and very exploitative. These persons, called
reformers, challenged the established church and developed
strong followings. Martin Luther, a reformer in Germany,
raised serious questions and was excommunicated from the
Catholic Church. His followers were called Lutherans. In
Switzerland, Ulrich Zwingli and John Calvin did not think
Luther had gone far enough with his changes, thus they
organized the Reformed Church. All these churches kept the
concept of a society built upon a close working relationship
between church and state and the practice of infant baptism.
The Lutherans continued the mass, although in a modified
form.

THE ANABAPTISTS

There were those who wished to go even further in change,
who opposed infant baptism, and who wanted to "reform the
reformers." They were called Anabaptists or "rebaptizers." A
small group in Zurich, Switzerland, began to study the scriptures seriously; they proposed further reforms to the heads of
the territorial (state) churches. Conrad Grebel, Felix Manz,
George Blaurock, and others—some of whom had been edu-
cated for the priesthood and who knew Latin, Greek, and
Hebrew—vigorously promoted reforms and were opposed
even more vigorously. Manz was publicly drowned, Grebel
died of the Plague at about 27 years of age, and Blaurock was
burned at the stake for his beliefs.

Michael Sattler who had been a prior at a Benedictine
monastery became an Anabaptist evangelist. In February
1527, Sattler presided over a secret conference which issued a
declaration of a "Brotherly Union." This declaration of seven
articles became known as the Schleitheim Articles which
embodied the Swiss Anabaptist view of Christian brotherhood. (These seven articles still provide basic guidelines in the

lives of the Mennonites and Amish today.)

MENNO SIMONS AND MENNONITES

Several years after the Schleitheim meeting a priest in the Netherlands, Menno Simons, joined the Anabaptist movement and became its most important evangelist in the sixteenth century. His followers were called "Mennists" or Mennonites, and the name was later adopted by the descendants of the Swiss Anabaptists who came to America. The teachings of Jesus as expressed in the Sermon on the Mount (Matthew 5:7) became the model for Mennonite belief and practice.

THE AMISH

The Amish emerged as a division of the Swiss Mennonites, namely the followers of Jakob Ammann, an elder of Markirch (Sainte Marie-Aux-Mines). He left Switzerland to become the spokesman for Mennonites in the Alsatian area. In July or August of 1693, Ammann made suggestions for more conservative practices than those followed by other Mennonite leaders, Hans Reist and Benedict Schneider. He insisted that those who were excommunicated from the group should be socially avoided (*Meidung*), and that the practice of foot washing should be initiated.

In Alsace most of the Mennonite congregations supported Ammann's views. Accordingly, the Mennonites in Switzerland, Alsace, and southern Germany were divided into two factions—Mennonites and Amish. Ammann's party attached great importance to strict discipline: wearing of traditional, simple clothing; avoidance of worldly grooming styles; beards were not to be trimmed, and mustaches were taboo. Later, hooks and eyes instead of buttons became one of the symbols of difference. Not only were excommunicated per-

sons to be avoided (shunned), but those members who associated with those who were banned were to be excommunicated. In some cases this separated husband from wife and children. The followers of Ammann were called Amish-Mennonites or simply Amish.

MENNONITES AND AMISH IN AMERICA

The first permanent Mennonite colony in America was established in 1683 at Germantown, Pennsylvania, several miles north of central Philadelphia. Although a few persons with Amish names came to America in the early eighteenth century, it was on October 8, 1737, that the ship *Charming Nancy* arrived and brought sufficient numbers of Amish to make an assembly or congregation possible. The periods of heaviest immigration were in 1737-1754 and again in the nineteenth century. These early settlements were located in Berks, Chester, and Lancaster counties of Pennsylvania.

Since Amish-Mennonite settlements in North America were widely separated and largely congregational in organization, practices became somewhat divergent. In order to reconcile such different cultural and religious practices, a General Ministers Conference was held in 1862. Unanimity was reached on certain major doctrines. All agreed that participation in war was contrary to the scriptures. However, many issues were not settled in further Amish Ministers Conferences held over the next sixteen years. The inability to agree brought these conferences to a close in 1878. At that time the congregations which favored maintaining the old traditions, with little or no change, became known as the Old Order Amish, the title used presently. These are the "house" Amish of today.

A more progressive group, of Alsatian origin, became the Evangelical Mennonites and the Central Conference of Mennonites—today, part of the General Conference Mennonite Church. The middle-of-the-road churches that favored moderate change continued as Amish-Mennonites. Most of the Illinois, Iowa, and Nebraska Mennonites today are of Amish-Mennonite background, as are many members in Indiana and Ohio. Many of these groups merged with the Mennonite Church between 1917 and 1925.

DEMOGRAPHY AND GEOGRAPHY

The Amish today live in twenty states and in the Canadian province of Ontario. A few are found in Central and South America. The baptized membership is 34,000, and the total Amish population is 86,000. Amish numbers continue to grow even though approximately 20 percent of the children do not follow the Amish faith. In 1890 there were 22 congregations or districts with 2,040 members in North America. The Amish nearly always live in closely knit concentrated geographical districts. Today the 86,000 are divided into 530 church districts. The states of Ohio (29,137), Pennsylvania (22,570), and Indiana (16,628) have 75 percent of the total population. Other states, and Ontario, with Amish populations of more than a thousand are: Missouri 2,560; Iowa 2,280, Wisconsin 2,280, Ontario 2,040, Illinois 1,690, Michigan 1,290, and New York 1,120. Still others are Maryland 970, Delaware 775, Minnesota 610, Kentucky 550, Kansas 520, Tennessee 410, Oklahoma 180, Montana 60, Arkansas 55, Florida 40, and Virginia 20.

The 530 Amish districts in North America average slightly less than 200 persons each in the larger population centers. The ratio between baptized to the unbaptized is 100 to 131. The average number of children per family is seven.

CHURCH ORGANIZATION

Each church district has a bishop, a deacon, and one or two ministers, generally selected by lot. These ordinations are for life and hold even though an ordained person may move to another Amish district. Services are held every two weeks at the home of a member. Some houses are arranged with movable partitions to better accommodate the whole congregation. In warm weather the service may be held in the driveway or a large barn. On the intervening Sunday other districts may be visited, or it may be a time of local visitation.

In the family structure children are taught strict obedience to parents, grandparents, and church authorities. All are taught that wisdom accumulates with age and that with age comes respect. The bishop in each district is clothed with great authority, and his decisions—with some input from other leaders—regulate day to day the social and religious ordering. The local regulations are part of the *ordnung* (rules). These understandings are verbally communicated. Historic agreements are in writing and clarify the basic principles of separation, nonresistance, apostasy, and exclusion.

AMISH RULES AND REGULATIONS (ORDNUNG)

All Amish groups accept the principle of being separate or different from the world, and each member makes a deep commitment to this principle at baptism. The methods or rules by which the principle of separation is carried out vary from church district to church district, even in those districts which may lie side by side. A church district generally consists of thirty to forty families, all sufficiently close geographically so they may reach the place of church services easily with a horse and buggy. Since the services are held in individual homes or barns, a district has to be restricted in size for all the members to meet in a home.

Even though certain rules may vary, members of individual congregations are not disturbed by different practices in other communities because there are some general norms upon which all Amish groups agree on for keeping out the world: no TV, no electricity, no telephones, no central heating or air-conditioning systems in homes, no automobiles, and no tractors with pneumatic tires. Women's uncut hair is covered with a head covering which is worn at all times. Men's hair is cut and worn to cover part of the ear. Mustaches are not allowed but they grow and keep beards after they are married.

Horses or mules are used for farming. No formal education beyond the eighth grade is required, but there are exceptions to the rule. More and more the Amish are conducting their own private schools and have benefited by a United States Supreme Court ruling which legalizes their own schools.

TRADITION AND ASSIMILATION

The Amish have lived in America for nearly two and a half centuries. They live segregated lives culturally but not geographically. They retain old world and early American customs, practices, and traditions, but an interesting phenomenon is the variations in application of historic patterns. Although the Amish do not use electricity, some have developed highly sophisticated applications of power from diesel engines. The "no automobile" rule does not keep the Amish from traveling. They extensively use public transportation and may hire drivers and cars or vans to take them where they want to go. Modern farming and husbandry information is put to good use. Farming operations are carried on with horse power, and often with the finest of horses. In northern Indiana and in other Amish communities, some of the finest pedigreed Belgian and Percheron horses are bred and raised by Amish farmers. In public sales some of these animals consigned by Amish farmers may bring $10,000 to $12,000 for a team (two), and the purchaser may be another Amish farmer.

The examples above may suggest that although the Amish seem to be changeless, they do accommodate to changes at the periphery. In this way they can remain true to their traditional way of life at the center.

PEN AND INK SKETCHES

The Amish people do not believe in personal photographs—"graven images." Nearly all personal pictures of the Amish we see today are taken with hidden cameras. In his effort to respect the tradition of "no picture-taking," Terry has created meticulous pen and ink drawings to depict Amish life and express his appreciation for his Amish roots.

Each of these pen and ink drawings represent many hours of careful study and application. These art forms are esthetically pleasing, precise in detail, and they correctly represent Amish patterns of life and making a living.

These impressive drawings cover such areas as transportation, farming methods and operations, farm equipment, farm buildings, houses (including housing for parents and grandparents), fields and gardens, food preservation (root cellar), school buildings, and children playing. In one sequence, the drawings show the construction of a barn, beginning with preparation of the frame-work and "laying out" the framework, plus the actual barn-raising.

In a very real sense, Terry L. Troyer, by using the medium of pen and ink, is truly in close keeping with the deeper Amish spirit itself. The end product is, consequently, an honest tribute to a great traditon which merits universal understanding.

Tilman R. Smith
Goshen, Indiana

The book, *Amish Society*, 3rd ed., completely revised, John Hopkins University Press, Baltimore, MD., 1980, was freely used for background information and facts.

The *Mennonite Encyclopedia*, Vol. I, Mennonite Publishing House, Scottdale, PA, 1955, was used as a source for its excellent historical data.

Amish women design and make most of the family's clothing. The clothes are modest and simply-made, using solid colors.

The typical work clothing for men is of blue denim material. Men wear straw hats in the summertime. For dress clothes they wear black suits with straight-cut collars and hooks and eyes instead of buttons. Their shirts may be blue, green, or lavender, but for dress, they are usually white. Black wide-brimmed hats are worn for dressy occasions and also during the cool seasons. Men have short and simple haircuts. They grow and keep beards after they are married.

The women are not permitted to wear slacks but must wear dresses which hang below the knee. Their dresses are dark-colored, most often lavender, green, blue, brown, gray, or black. They use only straight pins to fasten their clothes. As part of their religious beliefs, women do not cut their hair. They keep their heads covered at all times, showing reverence to God.

The children's clothes are patterned after their parents' clothing. They often wear lighter shades of green, blue, pink, and yellow.

Family unity is one of the main strongholds within the Amish society.

Buggies lined up neatly in a row make a typical scene at a large farm or community sale.

On warm days the side panels are rolled up, allowing the breezes to move through. At night, travel is made safer by attached kerosene lanterns, reflectors, and battery-operated blinkers.

Most of the communities have a small family buggy shop where the complete buggy is built.

The seat mounted on the buggy box will accommodate two or three people. The open buggy has a panel at the front for protection from mud and gravel kicked up by the horse's hooves. There is a storage space under the seat and a trunk at the rear. A small projecting roller, mounted on the edge of the buggy box, prevents the front wheels from damaging the buggy during sharp turns.

The wood framing of the "Double Buggy" will have black vinyl canvas stretched over it. The small framed areas on each side will support fixed windows. The chassis, which includes the under carriage, springs, and wheels, will be added after the body is completed.

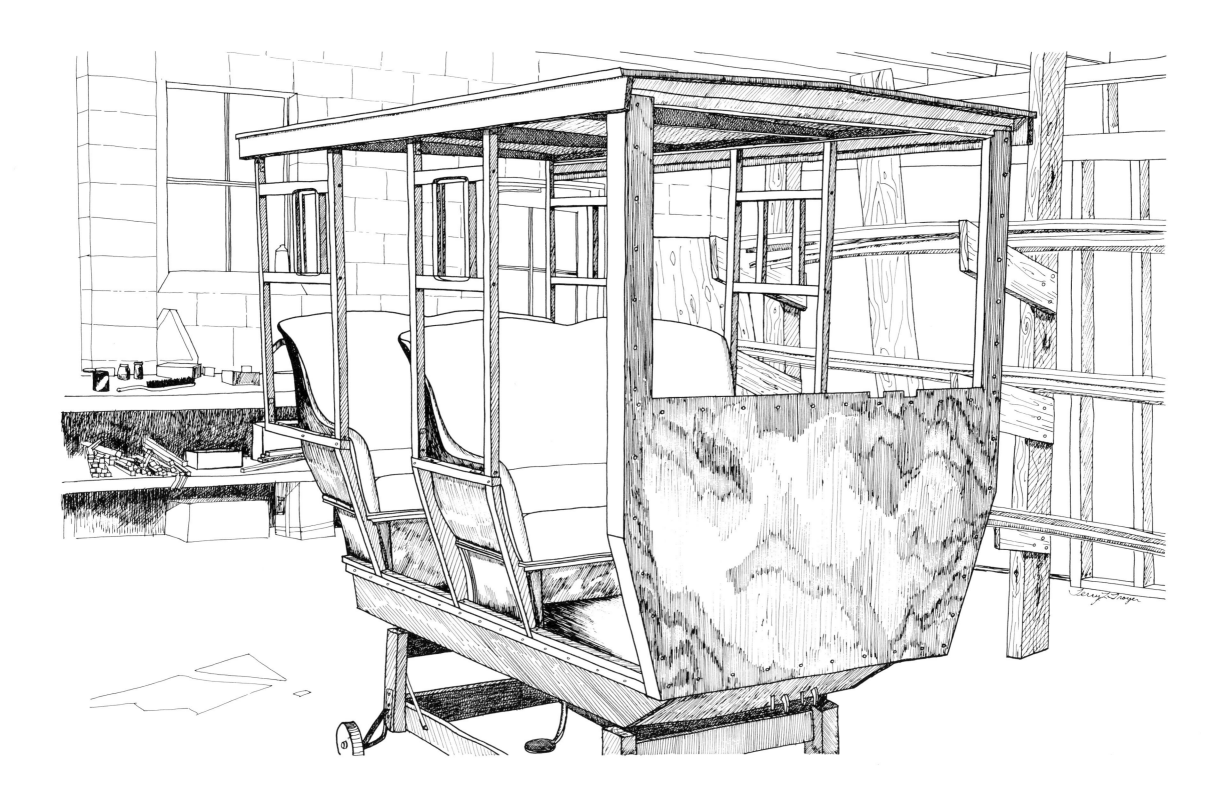

The "Double Buggy" is used as the family buggy. It seats four to six adults, plus children. Larger Amish families may have as many as ten people riding together in the same buggy.

In the cold winter months or during a heavy rain, the side panels are lowered and snapped securely to the frame.

The "Single Buggy" seats two to three people. All buggies have wooden wheels; some are rubber-rimmed and others are steel-rimmed.

The elderly usually have older driving horses which are not as energetic and are therefore easier to control.

The "Spring Wagon" is used as a pickup truck, and a similar one is used for a funeral hearse.

A wool blanket keeps the horse warm in cold weather while the owner may be attending an auction, visiting another family, or shopping in the community.

Travel in the winter is made easier by the sleigh. Heavy blankets are needed to keep warm.

Since the Amish do not have church buildings, they take turns meeting in each other's homes. A wagon containing portable church benches is moved from house to house for church services that are held every other Sunday.

The benches are of various lengths, having no backs on them. They are set up in the larger rooms of the house. While the men are seated in one room and the women in another, the preacher delivers his message by standing in a central doorway. The morning church service is always followed by a noon meal and an afternoon of fellowship and visiting.

The farm wagon, pulled by stocky work horses, is used by the Amish when they are threshing, husking corn, making hay, or transporting goods.

Amish farmers still have need for large storage barns. The hay, straw, corn fodder, and grain are all stored on the second level and are dropped down chutes for feeding the animals on ground level.

A typical Amish home often has a smaller grandfather (grossdaudy) house attached, allowing three generations to live and work together in harmony. Glass and screened sun porches provide a bright and cheerful atmosphere for the families.

The whole family usually works together in the garden. During the summer harvest season the women do the gardening while the men work long hours in the fields. The Amish garden organically, using animal manure from the farm for fertilizer.

The "Earth Cellar" is used for year-around storage of vegetables and fruits. The earth's protection provides an unchanging temperature, keeping food from freezing in the winter or spoiling in the summer. Double entry doors keep the temperature constant.

Bank barns provide easy access to both upper and lower levels. Hay, corn fodder, and straw are stored on the upper level, then are gravity fed to the cattle and horses in the lower level during the winter. The barns often have large straw sheds attached to them for additional storage.

Horses are an important part of farming. When a team of
six horses work to pull the disking rig, the four middle
horses, usually stocky draft horses, do the heavy pulling. The
two driving horses on each end, normally used for buggies,
provide additional power.

Young Amish boys help in preparing the fields for spring planting by driving a team of horses to pull farm equipment such as: a disking rig for turning the soil, a drill for sowing grain, and a manure spreader for spreading natural fertilizer on the field.

Corn planting is done with a two-row horse-drawn planter. It may take the farmer a full day to do what another farmer could do in a half hour with modern equipment.

The hay loader rakes up rows of cut hay and works it to the top with protruding prongs that move up and down. Once it reaches the top, the farmer spreads the hay over the wagon bed with pitchforks. After the wagon is stacked high, the hay is hauled to the barn for storage.

Amish boys return home on their work wagon after a long day of helping a neighbor make hay.

The horse-drawn binder cuts and binds grain in bundles for shocking. The carriage, a finger-like catch, collects and carries a group of bundles so they may be dropped off in rows.

The wheat shock is made by leaning six to eight bundles against each other. It is capped with two more bundles that are fanned out so that the rain will be shed from the grain heads.

The wheat shock allows the grain to cure and dry for two to three weeks before threshing begins.

During early harvest, wheat shocks dot the Amish country-side. Some of the typical buildings on their farms are the barn, corn crib, hog house, chicken house, and buggy and implement shed.

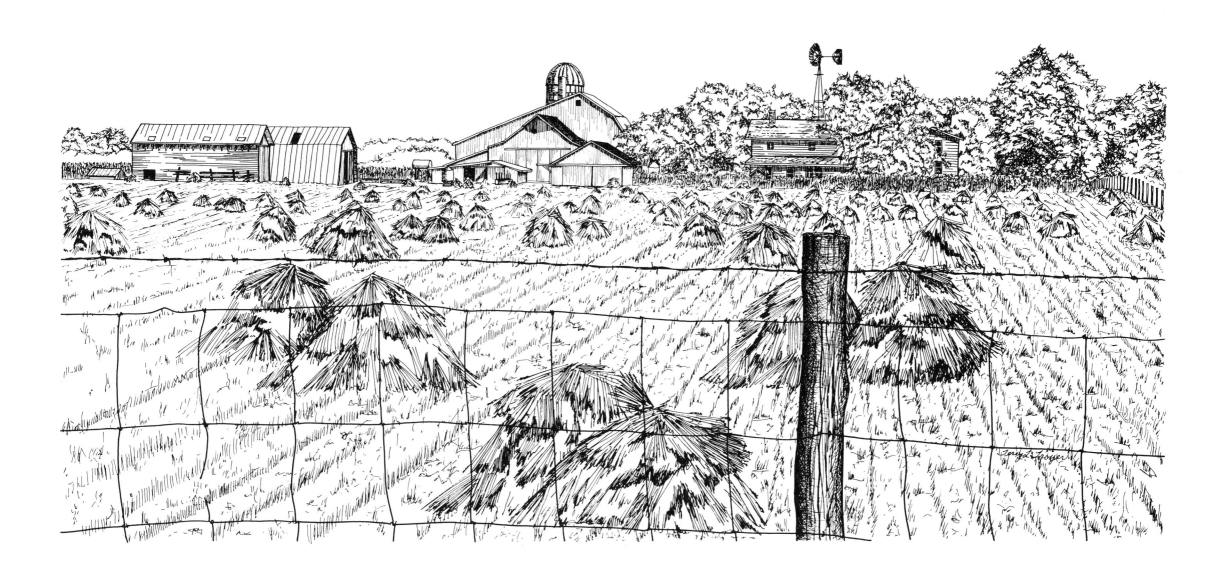

The threshing machine separates the grain from the chaff and straw. The straw is blown into a second-floor straw shed and used in the winter for bedding the cattle. The grain is dumped by a chute into a horse-drawn wagon and taken to be stored in the barn granary.

During the fall harvest, the corn is gathered together in corn shocks to dry. Each stalk is cut individually by stomping on it with a foot cutter. The foot cutter has a sharp projecting blade and is strapped to the shoe and leg. After the corn is dried it is husked, and the shocks (fodder) are hauled to the barn and stored for feeding cattle during the winter.

The white painted houses are simply furnished and have only draw shades to cover the windows.

Generally, the Amish farm is not complete without a windmill which pumps all the water for the farm's needs. At the base of the windmill is a milkhouse where the milk is stored and cooled by water drawn from the well.

For the most part, milking is done by hand. The milk is strained and poured into large cans which are then taken from the cow stable to the milkhouse on a wagon or pushcart.

Since the Amish do not use electricity, refrigerating the fresh milk is done in the "old way." The large milk cans are placed in cold running water to keep them chilled until the milk truck comes for the pickup.

Three Amish children . . . ready for school.

One-room schoolhouses have grades one through eight and are located in the immediate rural neighborhoods. The children's learning process begins at a young age at home and continues as they work on the family farm with their parents and grandparents. Reading, writing, and arithmetic are the main subjects that are taught. The Amish feel that an eighth grade education is sufficient for their needs.

Some children drive buggies to school. The horses are unhitched and kept in the horse barn during school hours.

On warm school days, at noon and at recess, barefoot children enjoy eating outside before playing on the teeter-totter, the swing, or at softball.

Outdoor toilets, "backhouses," are a common sight in most Amish school yards, since indoor plumbing is not standard in their schoolhouses.

Amish women enjoy making colorful quilts with many different patterns. The flower garden and star patterns are two
of the more popular designs.

Quilting has become a social event when neighboring
women get together for the day.

Since the Amish do not believe in using lightning rods, it is possible that during a summer electrical storm a barn may be struck and burned to the ground. Within a few weeks of such a loss, a portable sawmill is moved into the farmer's woods to begin cutting lumber for a new barn.

The saw blade is powered by connecting it to the drive shaft of a tractor.

Corner and flat chisels are used to carve out the mortises after the initial drilling of the heavy timbers.

The mortise will receive the tenon of another timber to form a strong joint which is then held in place by wooden pegs.

Heavy timbers are prepared for the barn-raising. Mortises, tenons, and peg holes are pre-cut, by hand, for easy assembling.

Wooden pegs are made for holding and pinning the barn timbers together. A long square piece of wood is first made pointed on one end by shaving it with a hand hatchet. A short piece of steel pipe is mounted on a heavy block of wood with a hole extending through it. A round peg is made by driving the pointed piece of wood into the pipe with a wooden mallet, shaving the edges as it passes through.

Within a month, timbers are ready for the barn-raising. Early in the morning, Amish friends and neighbors come together to help build a new barn. The Amish aid one another in times of need, no matter what the circumstances might be. This may range from hospital expenses to cleaning up and rebuilding after a disaster. This type of mutual aid eliminates insurance.

The day of the barn-raising is a family event. While the men work on the barn, some of the women prepare food for the noon meal. Other women sit under the shade trees and quilt, as well as watch the children play.

The barn begins to take shape just before the noon meal.
Although the Amishman in charge has only an eighth grade
education, he has many years of experience which enables
him to plan, design, and supervise the barn-raising.

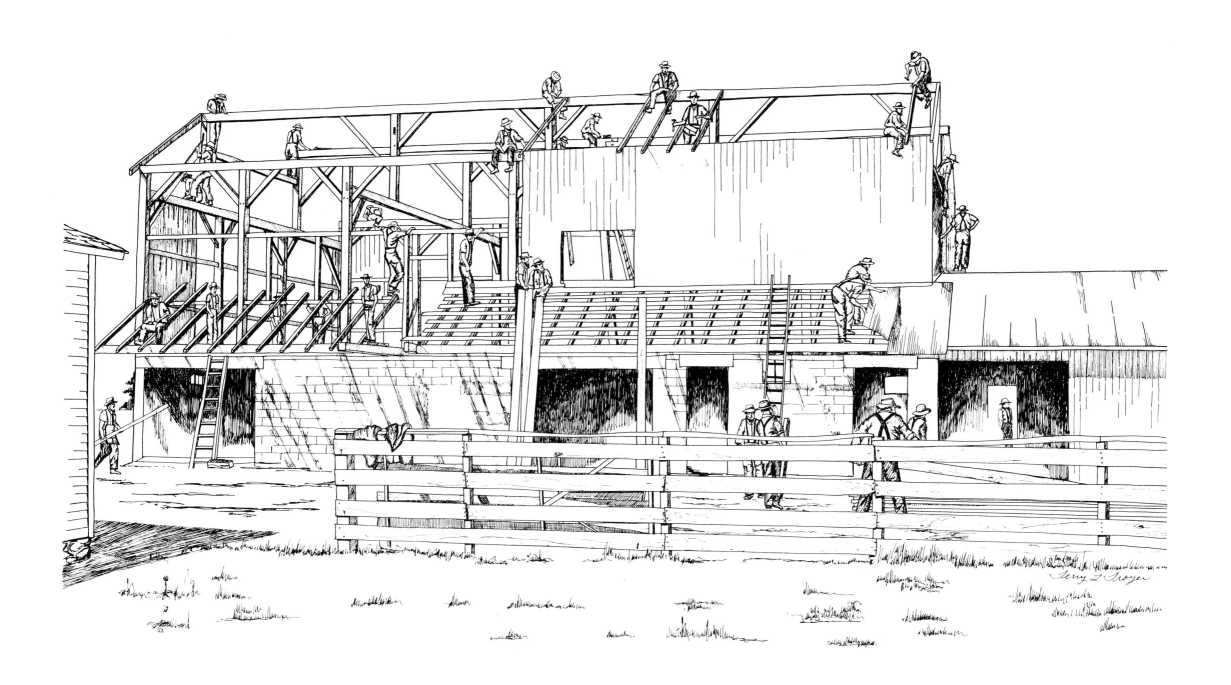

By mid-afternoon, the barn is nearly completed. The air is filled with the pounding of hammers striking nails and with the rasping of handsaws. Everyone works together in harmony as the roof is finished.

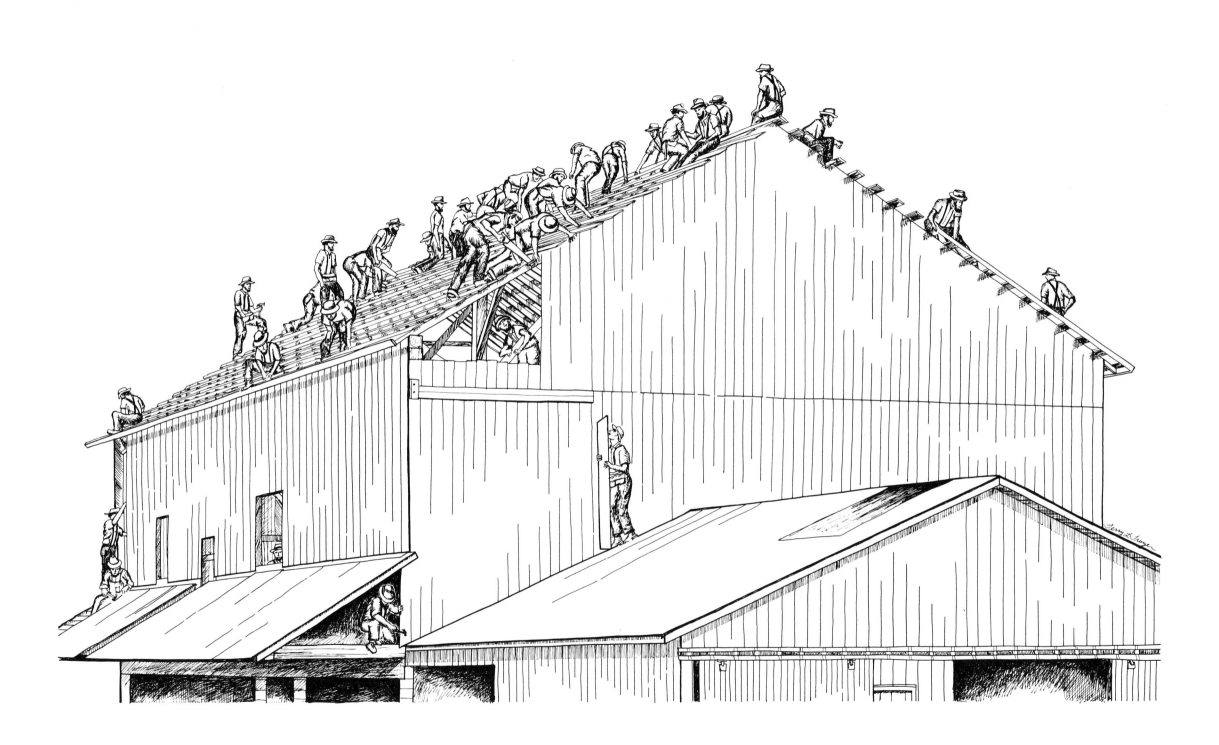

By late evening the doors are hung, and the area surrounding the barn is cleaned up. The barn is ready to receive the last cutting of hay for the summer . . . all in one day's work.